Air Fryer Toaster Oven Cookbook

Crispy, Quick and Easy Recipes to Delight Your Family and Friends With Mouth-Watering Meals

Mary Carton

Copyright © 2020 by Mary Carton

Legal Disclaimer

The information contained in this book and its contents is not designed to replace any form of medical or professional advice; and is not meant to replace the need for independent medical, financial, legal, or other professional advice or services that may be required. The content and information in this book have been provided for educational and entertainment purposes only.

The content and information contained in this book have been compiled from sources deemed reliable, and they are accurate to the best of the Author's knowledge, information, and belief. However, the Author cannot guarantee its accuracy and validity and therefore cannot be held liable for any errors and/or omissions. Further, changes are periodically made to this book as needed. Where appropriate and/or necessary, you must consult a professional (including but not limited to your doctor, attorney, financial advisor, or other such professional) before using any of the suggested remedies, techniques, and/or information in this book.

Upon using this book's contents and information, you agree to hold harmless the Author from any damages, costs, and expenses, including any legal fees potentially resulting from the application of any of the information in this book. This disclaimer applies to any loss, damages, or injury caused by the use and application of this book's contents, whether directly or indirectly, whether for breach of contract, tort, negligence, personal injury, criminal intent, or under any other circumstance.

You agree to accept all risks of using the information presented in this book.

You agree that by continuing to read this book, where appropriate and/or necessary, you shall consult a professional (including but not limited to your doctor, attorney, financial advisor, or other such professional) before using any of the suggested remedies, techniques, or information in this book.

Table of Contents

Round Ham Pin Wheels

Serving: 4

Prep Time: 10 minutes

Cook Time: 10 minutes

Ingredients:

- 1 sheet of pre-rolled puff pastry
- 4 handful of grated Gruyere cheese
- 4 teaspoon of Dijon mustard
- 6-8 slices of Parma ham

Directions:

1. Prepare a surface by flouring it up and add the pastry to your floured surface
2. Smear with mustard and add the ham
3. Sprinkle cheese on top
4. Roll it up from the shorter edge
5. Wrap up the wrapped up pastry using a Cling Film and place it in your fridge, allow it to chill for 30 minutes
6. Pre-heat your Toaster Oven to a temperature of 374 degrees Fahrenheit in Air Fry mode
7. Take the cooking basket and line it up with baking parchment

8. Place the pastry in the basket and slice it up into 1cm rounds

9. Slide the basket and cook for 10 minutes

10. Enjoy!

Nutritional Contents:

- Calories: 80
- Carbohydrate: 10g
- Protein: 4g
- Fat: 3g

Beef Salad With Nam Jim Dressing

Serving: 4

Prep Time: 10 minutes

Cook Time: 8 minutes

Ingredients:

Meatball Ingredients

- 16 ounce of grounded lamb
- 4 ounces of grounded turkey
- 1 ½ tablespoon of finely chopped parsley

- 1 teaspoon of grounded cumin
- 1 teaspoon of grounded coriander
- 1 teaspoon of cayenne pepper
- 1 teaspoon of red chili paste
- 2 cloves of finely chopped garlic
- ¼ cup of olive oil
- 1 teaspoon of salt
- 1 egg white

For the Mint Yogurt, you will need

- ½ a cup of non-fat Greek yogurt
- ¼ cup of sour cream
- 2 tablespoons of buttermilk
- ¼ cup of finely chopped mint
- 1 clove of finely chopped garlic
- 2 pinches of salt

Directions:

1. Pre-heat your Toaster Oven to a temperature of 390 degrees Fahrenheit in Air Fry mode

2. Take a large-sized bowl and add the listed ingredients for meatballs

3. Mix well and roll the mixture into balls

4. Smooth out the surface of the balls

5. Take your cooking basket and place the balls in the cooking basket

6. Allow them to cook for 8 minutes

7. Take another bowl and add the remaining ingredients under yogurt and mix them well to prepare your mint yogurt

8. Serve the cooked meatballs with the yogurt and a garnish of mint and olives

Nutritional Contents:

- Calories: 197
- Carbohydrate: 32g
- Protein: 7g
- Fat: 4g

Cheesy Bacon Croquettes

Serving: 4

Prep Time: 10 minutes

Cook Time: 30 minutes

Ingredients:

For the filling, you will need

- 1 pound of sharp cheddar
- 1 pound of thinly sliced bacon at room temperature

<u>For the breading, you will need</u>

- 4 tablespoon of olive oil
- 1 cup of all-purpose flour
- 2 beaten eggs
- 1 cup of seasoned breadcrumbs

Directions:

1. Cut your cheddar cheese blocks in equal-sized portions of 1 x 1 x ¾ inch portions

2. Take two pieces of bacon and cover the pieces with the cheddar, making sure that the whole cheese is engulfed with the bacon

3. Trim any excess fat

4. Take your wrapped cheese and place them in the fridge, chill for 15 minutes

5. Pre-heat your Toaster Oven to a temperature of 390 degrees Fahrenheit in Air Fry mode

6. Take a bowl and add oil and breadcrumbs and mix well

7. Dredge the wrapped-up cheese into your flour, eggs, and breadcrumbs

8. Press the breadcrumbs firmly to secure coating

9. Cook for about 7-8 minutes in your fryer

10. Enjoy!

Nutritional Contents:

- Calories: 170
- Carbohydrate: 47g
- Protein: 5g
- Fat: 10g

Bacon And Garlic Roast Potatoes

Serving: 4

Prep Time: 10 minutes

Cook Time: 30 minutes

Ingredients:

- 4 potatoes, peeled and halved
- 6 garlic cloves, squashed and peeled
- 4 streaky bacon, roughly cut
- 2 sprigs rosemary
- 1 tablespoon olive oil

Directions:

1. Take a bowl and add garlic, potatoes, bacon, and rosemary

2. Add oil and mix well

3. Pre-heat your Toaster Oven to a temperature of 392 degrees Fahrenheit in Air Fry mode

4. Transfer the processed potatoes to the cooking basket

5. Roast for 25-30 minutes

6. Enjoy!

Nutritional Contents:

- Calories: 418
- Carbohydrate: 65g
- Protein: 12g
- Fat: 13g

Lovely Beef Empanadas

Serving: 4

Prep Time: 10 minutes

Cook Time: 12 minutes

Ingredients:

- 8 thawed Goya empanada discs
- 1 cup of Picadillo
- 1 whisked egg white

- 1 teaspoon of water

Directions:

1. Pre-heat your Toaster Oven to a temperature of 325 degrees Fahrenheit in Air Fry mode

2. Spray the basket with cooking spray

3. Add about 2 tablespoons of Picadillo into the center of each of your disc

4. Fold the half using a fork and seal the edges

5. Repeat with any remaining dough

6. Carefully whisk egg whites with water

7. Brush the empanadas with this mixture

8. Bake for about 8 minutes (in batches of 3) until a golden color is seen

9. Enjoy!

Nutritional Contents:

- Calories: 263
- Fat: 17g
- Protein: 7g
- Dietary Fiber: 1g

Beef Herb Roast And Potato

Serving: 4

Prep Time: 10 minutes

Cook Time: 10 minutes

Ingredients:

- 2 teaspoon of olive oil
- 4 pound of top round roast beef
- 1 teaspoon of salt
- ¼ teaspoon of fresh ground black pepper

- 1 teaspoon of dried thyme
- ½ a teaspoon of finely chopped fresh rosemary
- 3 pound of halved red potatoes
- Olive oil freshly ground black pepper and salt

Directions:

1. Preheat your fryer to a temperature of 360 degrees Fahrenheit in Air Fry mode

2. Rub olive oil all over the beef

3. Take a bowl and add salt, thyme, pepper, rosemary and mix well

4. Season the beef with this mixture

5. Transfer the seasoned mix into Toaster Oven and cook for 20 minutes

6. Add potatoes with some oil and pepper

7. Turn the roast over and add the potatoes into the cooking basket

8. Cook for 20 minutes more

9. Make sure to rotate the roast for a few times

10. Cook until you have reached your desired temperature (130F for Rare, 140F for Medium and 160F for Well Done)

11. Allow it to cool for 5-10 minutes

12. Pre-heat your Toaster Oven temperature to 400 degrees Fahrenheit and keep cooking the potatoes for 8-10 minutes are browned

13. Shake and serve with the beef!

Nutritional Contents:

- Calories: 183
- Fat: 5g
- Protein: 11g
- Dietary Fiber: 1g

Tasty Beef And Broccoli

Serving: 4

Prep Time: 10 minutes

Cook Time: 12 minutes

Ingredients:

- ¾ pound of circular beef steak cut up into thin strips
- 1 pound of broccoli with stems removed and cut up into florets
- 1/3 cup of oyster sauce
- 2 teaspoon of sesame oil

- 1/3 cup of sherry
- 1 teaspoon of soy sauce
- 1 teaspoon of white sugar
- 1 teaspoon of cornstarch
- 1 tablespoon of olive oil
- 1 freshly sliced ginger root
- 1 garlic clove, minced

Directions:

1. Take a small-sized bowl and add oyster sauce, cornstarch, sesame oil, sherry, sugar, and soy sauce

2. Add the steak strips and marinate for 45 minutes

3. Pre-heat your Toaster Oven to 390 degrees F in Air Fry mode

4. Once the steak is ready, add them to the Toaster Oven cooking basket alongside broccoli

5. Add garlic, olive oil and ginger

6. Cook for about 12 minutes at 390 degrees Fahrenheit

7. Serve over rice

8. Enjoy!

Nutritional Contents:

- Calories: 338
- Carbohydrate: 50g
- Protein: 20g

Garlic Dredged Lamb Chops

Serving: 4

Prep Time: 10 minutes

Cook Time: 22 minutes

Ingredients:

- 1 garlic bulb
- 3 tablespoons olive oil
- 1 tablespoon oregano, chopped
- Fresh ground black pepper
- 8 lamb chops

Directions:

1. Pre-heat your Toaster Oven to 392 degrees Fahrenheit in Air Fry mode
2. Coat garlic bulb with olive oil and place it in your cooking basket
3. Roast for 12 minutes
4. Take a bowl and mix salt, olive oil, and pepper
5. Coat the lamb chops with ½ a tablespoon of the herb oil and allow to them to sit for 5 minutes
6. Pre-heat your Toaster Oven to 392 degrees Fahrenheit again and remove the roast garlic bulb
7. Place four lamb chops into the basket and slide the basket into the fryer
8. Cook for 5 minutes
9. Roast until the chops are nicely browned
10. Once done, keep them warm and repeat with the remaining chops
11. Squeeze garlic cloves between thumb and index finger over the herb oil
12. Add a bit of salt and pepper and stir well
13. Serve the chops with this garlic sauce
14. Enjoy!

Nutritional Contents:

- Calories: 171
- Carbohydrate: 0.4g
- Protein: 23g
- Fat: 8g

The Great Rib Eyes

Serving: 4

Prep Time: 10 minutes

Cook Time: 13 minutes

Ingredients:

- 2 pound of Ribeye Steak
- 1 tablespoon of Olive Oil
- Salt as needed
- Pepper as needed

Directions:

1. Pre-heat your Toaster Oven to a temperature of 356 degrees Fahrenheit in Air Fry mode

2. Rub oil all over the steak

3. Season the steak with salt and pepper

4. Place the steak onto your Toaster Oven and cook for 7 minutes

5. Turn the steak over and cook for about 6 minutes more

6. If needed, you may cook in small batches

7. Enjoy!

Nutritional Contents:

- Calories: 190
- Carbohydrate: 20g
- Protein: 24g
- Fat: 10g

Toasted Oven Burgers

Serving: 4

Prep Time: 10 minutes

Cook Time: 45 minutes

Ingredients:

- Onion as needed
- 10 ounce of Mixed Mince beef and pork

- 1 teaspoon of Garlic Puree
- 1 teaspoon of Tomato Puree
- 1 teaspoon of Mustard
- 1 teaspoon of Basil
- 1 teaspoon of mixed herbs
- Salt as needed
- Pepper as needed
- 4 pieces of bread buns
- Salad for burger toppings

Directions:

1. Take a mixing bowl and add the minced meat

2. Season well

3. Form four pieces of medium-sized burgers and place them to your Toaster Oven cooking basket

4. Cook for about 25 minutes on 390 degrees Fahrenheit in Air Fry mode

5. Cook for about 20 minutes further on 356 degrees Fahrenheit

6. Assemble the burger by placing the salad, cheese, and bun

7. Serve and enjoy!

Nutritional Contents:

- Calories: 359
- Carbohydrate: 15g
- Protein: 18g
- Fat: 31g

Roaster Sirloin Steak

Serving: 4

Prep Time: 10 minutes

Cook Time: 15 minutes

Ingredients:

- 4 small potatoes, chopped
- 1 tablespoon of Olive oil
- 1 teaspoon of Cayenne pepper
- 1 teaspoon of Italian herbs
- 1 teaspoon of Salt

- 70 ounce of Sirloin steak
- ½ a tablespoon of olive oil
- Salt as needed
- Pepper as needed

Directions:

1. Take a medium-sized bowl and add olive oil, potatoes, Italian herbs, cayenne pepper and salt
2. Mix well
3. Pre-heat your Toaster Oven to 356 degrees Fahrenheit in Air Fry mode
4. Place the potatoes in your Toaster Oven basket and cook for 16 minutes
5. Make sure to give the potatoes a toss halfway through
6. Once done, keep it on the side
7. Rub the steak with pepper, oil, and salt
8. Place the steak into your fryer and cook for 7-13 minutes at 392 Fahrenheit depending on your doneness
9. Serve with roasted potatoes, enjoy!

Nutritional Contents:

- Calories: 135
- Carbohydrate: 0g
- Protein: 23g
- Fat: 5g

Coffee Rubbed Rib Eye

Serving: 4

Prep Time: 10 minutes

Cook Time: 12 minutes

Ingredients:

- ¼ cup of ancho chili powder
- ¼ cup of espresso powder
- 2 tablespoons of paprika
- 2 tablespoons of dark brown sugar

- 1 tablespoon of dry mustard
- 1 tablespoon of kosher salt
- 1 tablespoon of black pepper
- 1 tablespoon of ground coriander
- 1 tablespoon of dried oregano
- 2 teaspoon of Aleppo pepper
- 4 pieces of boneless rib-eye steak
- Salt as needed
- Pepper as needed
- 10 ounces of fries

Directions:

1. Pre-heat your Toaster Oven to a temperature of 392 degrees Fahrenheit in Air Fry mode

2. Rub the mixture over your steak

3. Season with some salt and pepper

4. Allow it to sit for 20 minutes

5. Cook for about 10 minutes in your Toaster Oven, flip it and cook for 10 minutes more

6. Keep repeating the process with your remaining steaks

7. Once done, remove the steak and place it to your serving platter

8. Pre-heat your Toaster Oven to 392 degrees Fahrenheit again and place the fries in the basket

9. Cook for a few minutes, making sure to give the fries a shake about halfway through

10. Serve with the Steak

11. Enjoy!

Nutritional Contents:

- Calories: 557
- Carbohydrate: 2g
- Protein: 69g
- Fat: 29g

Mushroom Meat Steak And Wedges

Serving: 4

Prep Time: 10 minutes

Cook Time: 12 minutes

Ingredients:

- 3 tablespoon of Coconut Ghee
- 10 ounce of Fillet steak
- 1 large-sized potato
- 2 ounce of Button Mushrooms

- 2 tablespoons of Coconut Milk
- 1 teaspoon of garlic cloves grated
- 1 teaspoon of parsley
- 1 teaspoon of mustard powder
- Just a pinch of oregano
- Salt as needed
- Pepper as needed
- Mustard Mayo mix

Directions:

1. Chop up your mushrooms into medium-sized slices
2. Wash them thoroughly
3. Chop up the potatoes into wedges and wash them well
4. Rub the fillet with pepper, salt, and parsley
5. Using a pastry brush, brush 1 tablespoon of coconut ghee all over the steak
6. Place the potato wedges into the Toaster Oven and cook for 10 minutes at 356 degrees Fahrenheit alongside 1 tablespoon of oil in Air Fry mode
7. Take a small-sized mixing bowl and add 2 tablespoons of coconut ghee, garlic and coconut milk alongside the remaining seasoning
8. Mix well and add the mushroom to one side
9. Add this to the fryer, placing it just beside your potatoes and cook for 8 minutes more

10. Remove the steak and allow it to cool

11. Cook the mushrooms in the sauce for about 5 minutes more

12. Remove the potatoes and mushrooms sauce and pour it over the steak

13. Serve with some mustard mayo if preferred

14. Enjoy!

Nutritional Contents:

- Calories: 283
- Carbohydrate: 14g
- Protein: 2g
- Fat: 25g

Gravy And Fried Steak

Serving: 4

Prep Time: 10 minutes

Cook Time: 15 minutes

Ingredients:

- 6 ounce of sirloin steak
- 3 beaten eggs
- 1 cup of flour
- 1 cup of panko

- 1 teaspoon of onion powder
- 1 teaspoon of garlic powder
- 1 teaspoon of salt
- 1 teaspoon of pepper

Gravy

- 6 ounce of ground sausage meat
- 2 tablespoons of flour
- 2 cups of milk
- 1 teaspoon of pepper

Directions:

1. Season the panko with spices

2. Dredge your steak in the flour, followed by the egg and finally the panko

3. Place your breaded steak in the cooking basket

4. Spray it with some cooking spray

5. Pre-heat your Fryer to 360 degrees Fahrenheit in Air Fry mode

6. Place your steak and cook for 6 minutes

7. Once done, remove and cut it up into 2 pieces

8. Take a pan and place it over medium heat

9. Add sausage until cooked well

10. Drain the fat and reserve 2 tablespoons of grease

11. Add flour into the pan with sausage and mix well until it is incorporated well

12. Slow mix in milk and stir well over medium heat until the milk is thick

13. Serve the steak with this gravy

14. Enjoy!

Nutritional Contents:

- Calories: 660
- Carbohydrate: 29g
- Protein: 38g
- Fat: 43g

The Bison Steak

Serving: 4

Prep Time: 10 minutes

Cook Time: 15 minutes

Ingredients:

- 2 pound of bison sirloin steak
- 1 tablespoon of Montreal Steak Seasoning
- 1 tablespoon of oil

Directions:

1. Pre-heat your Toaster Oven to a temperature of 400 degrees Fahrenheit in Air Fry mode

2. Add oil to your skillet

3. Allow the skillet to heat up

4. Pat the seasoning all around the bison

5. Sear both sides of the steak

6. Bake your steak in the Toaster Oven for about 15 minutes until the internal temperature reaches 140 degrees Fahrenheit

7. Remove it

8. Seal the steak in your cast iron skillet with an Aluminum foil

9. Allow it to rest for 15 minutes

10. Slice it up and enjoy it!

Nutritional Contents:

- Calories: 141
- Carbohydrate: 32g
- Protein: 28g
- Fat: 3g

Coffee Dressed T-Bone Steak

Serving: 4

Prep Time: 10 minutes

Cook Time: 12 minutes

Ingredients:

- ¼ cup of coffee
- 2 tablespoons of brown sugar
- 3 tablespoons of butter

- 1 and ½ pound of Bone in Steak

Directions:

1. Prepare your steak by taking it out the fridge and allow it to rest for 30 minutes on a counter

2. Prepare your dry rub by taking a bowl and mixing ¼ cup of coffee and 2 tablespoons of brown sugar

3. Pre-heat your Toaster Oven to 400 degrees Fahrenheit for about 5 minutes in Air Fry mode

4. Transfer your steak to the cooking basket and cook for about 4 minutes (one side, making sure to add 1 tablespoon of butter after 2 minutes

5. Flip it up

6. Add another 1 tablespoon of butter

7. Cook for 3 minutes more

8. Take the steak out and place it on a grill

9. Allow it to cool

10. Slice it up and enjoy it!

Nutritional Contents:

- Calories: 130
- Carbohydrate: 5g
- Protein: 24g
- Fat: 5g

Toaster Oven Burger

Serving: 4

Prep Time: 10 minutes

Cook Time: 15 minutes

Ingredients:

- 1 tablespoon of Worcestershire sauce
- 1 teaspoon of Maggi seasoning sauce
- Just a few drops of liquid smoke
- ½ a teaspoon of garlic powder

- ½ a teaspoon of onion powder
- ½ a teaspoon of salt substitute
- ½ a teaspoon of ground black pepper
- ½ a teaspoon of dried oregano
- 1 teaspoon of dried parsley
- 1 pound of uncooked 93% lean ground beef

Directions:

1. Spray your cooking basket with some cooking spray

2. Pre-heat the temperature of your fryer to 350 degrees Fahrenheit in Air Fry mode

3. Take a small-sized bowl and mix the seasoning ingredients, starting from Worcestershire sauce down to dried parsley

4. Add beef to the mix

5. Mix well making sure not to overwork the meat

6. Divide the mixture into 4 patties and shape them, use your thumb to put an indent in the center of each patty

7. Place them in your Toaster Oven in batches if needed and cook for 10 minutes (for medium)

8. Serve between hot buns and some salad

9. Enjoy!

Nutritional Contents:

- Calories: 400
- Carbohydrate: g
- Protein: 92g
- Fat: 15g

Ham And Pineapple Steak

Serving: 4

Prep Time: 10 minutes

Cook Time: 10 minutes

Ingredients:

- 1 ham steak
- 7 pineapple pieces
- 5 cubes feta
- 1 sprinkle of cheese, grated

- Pepper as needed
- 1 slice of cheese

Directions:

1. Pre-heat your Toaster Oven 356-degree Fahrenheit in Air Fry mode

2. Add the ham and cook it for about 10 minutes, making sure to pull out to cooking basket at 5 minutes mark and add cheese, followed by feta, and pineapple

3. Push it back and cook for remaining 5 minutes

4. Sprinkle with a bit of pepper

5. Serve and enjoy!

Nutritional Contents:

- Calories: 258
- Carbohydrate: 24g
- Protein: 24g
- Fat: 8g

Sriracha Beef Satay

Serving: 4

Prep Time: 10 minutes

Cook Time: 8 minutes

Ingredients:

- ¼ cup roasted peanuts, chopped
- ½ cup cilantro, chopped
- 1 teaspoon ground coriander
- 1 teaspoon sriracha sauce
- 1 tablespoon sugar
- 1 tablespoon garlic, minced
- 1 tablespoons ginger, minced
- 1 tablespoons soy sauce
- 1 tablespoon fish sauce
- 2 tablespoon oil
- 1 pound beef shank flank steak, sliced

Directions:

1. Whisk fish sauce with ginger, garlic, soy sauce, oil, sugar, coriander, ¼ cup cilantro, and sriracha in a mixing bowl. Toss- in the beef strips and mix well to coat.

2. Cover the beef and refrigerate for 30 minutes. Place the beef in the Air Fryer basket.

3. Set the Air Fryer basket inside the Air Fryer toaster oven and close the lid. Select the Air Fry mode at 400 degrees F temperature for 8 minutes.

4. Flip the beef slices and continue cooking. Garnish with peanuts and cilantro. Serve warm.

Nutritional Contents:

- Calories: 390
- Fat: 13g
- Carbohydrates: 8g
- Protein: 41g

Quinoa Fried Beef

Serving: 4

Prep Time: 10 minutes

Cook Time: 23 minutes

Ingredients:

- 3 cups quinoa cooked and cold
- 1 cup frozen peas, carrots
- 6 tablespoons soy sauce
- 1 tablespoon oil
- 1 cup onion, diced
- 1 cup beef cubes

Directions:

1. Mix quinoa, vegetable oil, and soy sauce in a bowl. Toss in carrots, beef cubes, onion, and peas.
2. Spread this beef mixture in a baking pan. Set the baking pan inside the Air Fryer toaster oven and close the lid.
3. Select the baking mode at 360 degrees F temperature for 20 minutes.
4. Toss the beef after 10 minutes then resume cooking. Serve warm.

Nutritional Contents:

- Calories: 204
- Fat: 9g
- Carbohydrates: 24g
- Protein: 15g

Raspberry Glazed Pork Chops

Serving: 4

Prep Time: 10 minutes

Cook Time: 23 minutes

Ingredients:

- 1 tablespoon orange juice
- 2 tablespoon seedless raspberry jam
- 2 tablespoons brown sugar
- 1/3 cup balsamic vinegar
- ¼ cup all-purpose flour
- 4 smoked bone-pork chops
- 1 cup pecans, chopped
- 1 cup panko breadcrumbs
- ¼ cup 2% milk
- 2 large whole eggs

Directions:

1. Beat eggs with milk in a shallow tray. Mix breadcrumbs with pecans on another plate.
2. Spread the flour in a bowl. First coat the flour with pork chops then dip them in the eggs.

3. Coat them well with the breadcrumbs then place them in the Air Fryer basket.
4. Spray the chops with cooking oil. Set the Air Fryer basket inside the Air Fryer toaster oven and close the lid.
5. Select the Air Fry mode at 350 degrees F temperature for 15 minutes. Flip the chops after 7 minutes of cooking then continue cooking. Meanwhile, mix jam with vinegar, juice, and sugar in a saucepan.
6. Stir cook for 8 minutes until it thickens. Pour this sauce over the cooked chops and serve.

Nutritional Contents:

- Calories: 537
- Fat: 6g
- Carbohydrates: 5g
- Protein: 37g

Awesome Beef Burgers

Serving: 4

Prep Time: 10 minutes

Cook Time: 15 minutes

Ingredients:

- 4 hamburger buns
- ½ tablespoon mustard
- 4 lettuce leaves
- 1 tablespoon pickles
- ½ cup tomato, sliced
- ½ cup onion, sliced
- 4 slices sharp cheddar
- ¼ tablespoon black pepper
- 4 ground beef patties

Directions:

1. The beef patties are rubbed with black pepper.
2. The air fryer toaster oven should be preheated at 375F for 5 min.
3. The basket should be covered by aluminum foil. The patties are placed in the basket and heated for 10 min with intermittent flipping.

4. One slice of cheese is placed on each patty and heated for another 2 min.
5. One cooked patty is placed on one bun to which are added lettuce leaves, pickles, onion, and mustard and covered by another bun.
6. Serve and enjoy!

Nutritional Contents:

- Calories: 240
- Fat: 6g
- Carbohydrates: 11g
- Protein: 16g

Beef And Cheese Enchiladas

Serving: 4

Prep Time: 10 minutes

Cook Time: 10 minutes

Ingredients:

- 1 pound ground beef
- 1 tablespoon taco seasoning
- 8 gluten-free tortillas
- 1 can black beans, rinsed
- 1 can tomatoes, diced
- 1 can green chilies, chopped
- 1 cup Mexican cheese, shredded
- 1 cup cilantro, chopped
- ½ cup sour cream

Directions:

1. The ground beef should be cooked in a frying pan till brown.
2. Taco seasonings should cover the cooked beef.
3. The tomatoes, beans, chilies should be added to the beef and mixed thoroughly.

4. The mixture is used to cover the tortillas followed by enchiladas sauce. The Toasted Oven should be preheated at 355F for 5 min.

5. The tortillas are placed in the basket, and topping is done by cheese. They are heated for 6 min with intermittent flipping.

6. The cooked tortillas are removed from the basket, topped with cilantro and cream, and served hot.

Nutritional Contents:

- Calories: 454
- Fat: 8g
- Carbohydrates: 40g
- Protein: 26g

Asian Vegetable With Beef

Serving: 4

Prep Time: 10 minutes

Cook Time: 10 minutes

Ingredients:

- ¼ cup of water
- 1/3 cup brown sugar
- ¼ cup of rice vinegar
- 1 tablespoon sesame oil
- ½ cup of soy sauce
- 2 tablespoons ginger, grated
- 1 tablespoon garlic, minced
- ½ yellow onion, sliced
- 1 red pepper, sliced
- 2 tablespoons corn starch
- 1 pound sirloin steak

Directions:

1. The steak should be cut into strips.
2. All the ingredients are mixed thoroughly to form a mixture of the marinade.

3. The steak strips are placed inside a zip bag to which is added the mixture is added and kept in the refrigerator overnight to marinade.

4. The steak pieces are removed from the bag by tongs and placed in the cutting board for 5 min.

5. The air fryer toaster oven should be preheated at 390 F for 5 min. The basket should be covered by aluminum foil.

6. The steaks are placed in the basket and heated for 6 min with intermittent flipping.

7. The cooked steaks are removed from the basket, garnished with scallions and sesame seeds, and served hot.

Nutritional Contents:

- Calories: 289
- Fat: 7g
- Carbohydrates: 27g
- Protein: 31g

Greek Lamb Chops

Serving: 4

Prep Time: 10 minutes

Cook Time: 15 minutes

Ingredients:

- 8 loin lamb chops
- 2 tablespoons olive oil
- 4 tablespoons spoony grainy mustard
- ¼ tablespoon pepper
- ¼ tablespoon salt
- 1 tablespoon thyme

Directions:

1. The mustard, thyme, oregano, and olive oil are mixed thoroughly in a bowl. The lamb chops should be rinsed and dried.
2. The prepared mixture is coated on the lamb chops.
3. The air fryer toaster oven should be preheated at 390 F for 5 min. The lambs are placed assembled pan into rack Position and heated for 15 min with intermittent flipping.

4. The cooked lamb should be removed from the basket and served hot.

Nutritional Contents:

- Calories: 265
- Fat: 40g
- Carbohydrates: 4g
- Protein: 30g

Fajita Steak

Serving: 4

Prep Time: 10 minutes

Cook Time: 15 minutes

Ingredients:

- 4 tortilla
- 1 pack Fajita seasoning
- 1 tablespoon olive oil
- ½ cup white onions, sliced
- 1 yellow bell pepper, sliced
- 1 red bell pepper, sliced
- 1 green bell pepper, sliced
- 1 pound thinly cut steaks

Directions:

1. The steak pieces should be thinly sliced.
2. The steak pieces should be coated with pepper and onion, followed by Fajita seasoning.
3. Put the assembled pan into rack Position
4. Set the oven to Air Fry at 400°F for 10 minutes. The cooked steaks are removed from the oven and allowed to stand for 10 min and served hot in warm tortillas.

Nutritional Contents:

- Calories: 305
- Fat: 14g
- Carbohydrates: 15g
- Protein: 22g

Ham Glazed In Fresh Brown Sugar

Serving: 4

Prep Time: 10 minutes

Cook Time: 55 minutes

Ingredients:

- 1 pound ground pork
- ¼ tablespoon pepper
- ¼ tablespoon salt
- 4 sharp cheddar cheese,
- 1 tablespoon pickles

Directions:

1. The ingredients for glazing are mixed and heated until the sugar melts.
2. The ham should be scored with a knife. The hams are dipped in the mixture for proper coating.
3. The air fryer oven toaster should be preheated at 390 F for 5 min. The basket should be covered by aluminum foil.
4. The hams are placed in the basket and heated for 20 min with intermittent flipping.

5. The hams are again brushed with the glaze mixture and further heated for another 30 min.

6. The above procedure is repeated and heated for another 5 min.

7. Let the ham stand for 5 minutes, serve and enjoy!

Nutritional Contents:

- Calories: 370
- Fat: 72g
- Carbohydrates: 8g
- Protein: 18g

Pork Belly Bites BBQ Sauce

Serving: 4

Prep Time: 10 minutes

Cook Time: 23 minutes

Ingredients:

- 1./2 tablespoon garlic powder
- ¼ cup BBQ sauce
- ¼ tablespoon pepper
- ¼ tablespoon salt
- 1 pound pork belly
- 1 tablespoon soy sauce

Directions:

1. The skin should be removed from the pork belly and cut into small cubes. The cubes are put in a bowl and rubbed with salt, pepper, and garlic powder and soy sauce for proper coating.
2. The air fryer toaster oven should be preheated at 390 F for 5 min.
3. The basket should be covered by aluminum foil.

4. The pork cubes are placed in the basket and heated for 15 min with intermittent flipping until they turn tender.
5. Let the cubes stand for 5 minutes and soak in BBQ sauce
6. Enjoy!

Nutritional Contents:

- Calories: 600
- Fat: 18g
- Carbohydrates: 75g
- Protein: 18g

Blackberry Chicken Wings

Serving: 4

Prep Time: 35 minutes

Cook Time: 50minutes

Ingredients:

- 3 pounds chicken wings, about 20 pieces
- ½ cup blackberry chipotle jam
- Sunflower seeds and pepper to taste
- ½ cup of water

Directions:

1. Add water and jam to a bowl and mix well

2. Place chicken wings in a zip bag and add two-thirds of marinade

3. Season with sunflower seeds and pepper

4. Let it marinate for 30 minutes

5. Pre-heat your Toaster Oven to 400-degree F in bake mode

6. Prepare a baking sheet and wire rack, place chicken wings in a wire rack and bake for 15 minutes

7. Brush remaining marinade and bake for 30 minutes more

8. Enjoy!

Nutritional Contents:

- Calories: 502
- Fat: 39g
- Carbohydrates: 01.8g
- Protein: 34g

Lovely Herbed Chicken Breast

Serving: 2

Prep Time: 10 minutes

Cook Time: 40 minutes

Ingredients:

- 1/2 tablespoon dry parsley
- 1/2 tablespoon dry basil
- 2 chicken breast halves, boneless and skinless
- 1/4 teaspoon sunflower seeds
- 1/4 teaspoon red pepper flakes, crushed
- 1 tomato, sliced

Directions:

1. Pre-heat your Toaster Oven to 350 degrees F in bake mode

2. Take a 9x13 inch baking dish and grease it up with cooking spray.

3. Sprinkle 1 tablespoon of parsley, 1 teaspoon of basil, and spread the mixture over your baking dish.

4. Arrange the chicken breast halves over the dish and sprinkle garlic slices on top.

5. Take a small bowl and add 1 teaspoon parsley, 1 teaspoon of basil, sunflower seeds, basil, red pepper, and mix well. Pour the mixture over the chicken breast.

6. Top with tomato slices and cover, bake for 25 minutes.

7. Remove the cover and bake for 15 minutes more.

8. Serve and enjoy!

Nutritional Contents:

- Calories: 150
- Fat: 4g
- Carbohydrates: 4g
- Protein: 25g

Bacon And Chicken Garlic Wrap

Serving: 4

Prep Time: 15 minutes

Cook Time: 10 minutes

Ingredients:

- 1 chicken fillet, cut into small cubes
- 8-9 thin slices bacon, cut to fit cubes
- 6 garlic cloves, minced

Directions:

1. Pre-heat your Toaster Oven to 400-degree F in toast mode

2. Line a baking tray with aluminum foil

3. Add minced garlic to a bowl and rub each chicken piece with it

4. Wrap bacon piece around each garlic chicken bite

5. Secure with toothpick

6. Transfer bites to the baking sheet, keeping a little bit of space between them

7. Toast for about 15-20 minutes until crispy

8. Serve and enjoy!

Nutritional Contents:

- Calories: 260
- Fat: 19g
- Carbohydrates: 5g
- Protein: 22g

Amazingly Baked Chicken Breast

Serving: 2

Prep Time: 10 minutes

Cook Time: 40 minutes

Ingredients:

- 2 pieces of 8 ounces skinless and boneless chicken breast
- Salt and pepper as needed
- ¼ cup of olive oil and lemon juice (equal amount)
- ½ a teaspoon of dried oregano
- ¼ teaspoon of dried thyme

Directions:

1. Season breast by rubbing salt and pepper on all sides
2. Transfer the chicken to a bowl
3. Take another bowl and add olive oil, oregano, lemon juice, thyme and mix well
4. Pour the prepared marinade over the chicken breast and allow it to marinate for 10 minutes
5. Pre-heat your Toaster Oven to 400 degrees Fahrenheit in bake mode

6. Set the Toaster Oven rack about 6 inches above the heat source

7. Transfer the chicken breast to a baking sheet and pour extra marinade on top

8. Bake for 35-45 minutes until the center is no longer pink

9. Remove it and place it on the top rack

10. Broil for 5 minutes more

11. Enjoy and serve!

Nutritional Contents:

- Calories: 501
- Fat: 32g
- Carbohydrates: 3.5g
- Protein: 47g

Healthy Chicken Cream Salad

Serving: 3

Prep Time: 5 minutes

Cook Time: 50 minutes

Ingredients:

- 2 chicken breasts
- 1 and ½ cups cashew cream
- 3 ounces celery
- 2-ounce green pepper, chopped
- ½ ounce green onion, chopped
- ½ cup mayonnaise, homemade
- 3 hard-boiled eggs, chopped

Directions:

1. Pre-heat your Toaster Oven to 350 degrees F in bake mode

2. Take a baking sheet and place chicken, cover with cream

3. Bake for 30-40 minutes

4. Take a bowl and mix in chopped celery, peppers, onions

5. Chop baked chicken into bite-sized portions

6. Peel and chop hard-boiled eggs

7. Take a large salad bowl and mix in eggs, veggies, and chicken

8. Toss well and serve

9. Enjoy!

Nutritional Contents:

- Calories: 415
- Fat: 24g
- Carbohydrates: 4g
- Protein: 40g

The Blackened Chicken

Serving: 4

Prep Time: 10 minutes

Cook Time: 10 minutes

Ingredients:

- ½ teaspoon paprika
- 1/8 teaspoon salt
- ¼ teaspoon cayenne pepper
- ¼ teaspoon ground cumin
- ¼ teaspoon dried thyme
- 1/8 teaspoon ground white pepper
- 1/8 teaspoon onion powder
- 2 chicken breasts, boneless and skinless

Directions:

1. Pre-heat your Toaster Oven to 350-degree Fahrenheit in bake mode

2. Grease baking sheet

3. Take a cast-iron skillet and place it over high heat

4. Add oil and heat it for 5 minutes until smoking hot

5. Take a small bowl and mix salt, paprika, cumin, white pepper, cayenne, thyme, onion powder

6. Oil the chicken breast on both sides and coat the breast with the spice mix

7. Transfer to your hot pan and cook for 1 minute per side

8. Transfer to your prepared baking sheet and bake for 5 minutes

9. Serve and enjoy!

Nutritional Contents:

- Calories: 136
- Fat: 3g
- Carbohydrates: 1g
- Protein: 24g

Almond butternut Chicken

Serving: 4

Prep Time: 15 minutes

Cook Time: 30 minutes

Ingredients:

- ½ pound Nitrate free bacon
- 6 chicken thighs, boneless and skinless
- 2-3 cups almond butternut squash, cubed
- Extra virgin olive oil
- Fresh chopped sage
- Sunflower seeds and pepper as needed

Directions:

1. Prepare your Toaster Oven by preheating it to 425 degrees F in Bake Mode

2. Take a large skillet and place it over medium-high heat, add bacon and fry until crispy

3. Take bacon and place it on the side, crumbled the bacon

4. Add cubed almond butternut squash in the bacon grease and Sauté, season with sunflower seeds and pepper

5. Once the squash is tender, remove skillet and transfer to a plate

6. Add coconut oil to the skillet and add chicken thigh, cook for 10 minutes

7. Season with sunflower seeds and pepper

8. Remove skillet from the stove and transfer to Toaster Oven

9. Bake for 12-15 minutes, top with crumbled bacon and sage

10. Enjoy!

Nutritional Contents:

- Calories: 136
- Fat: 3g
- Carbohydrates: 1g
- Protein: 24g

Parmesan Baked Chicken

Serving: 2

Prep Time: 5 minutes

Cook Time: 20 minutes

Ingredients:

- 2 tablespoons ghee
- 2 boneless chicken breasts, skinless
- Pink sunflower seeds
- Freshly ground black pepper
- ½ cup mayonnaise, low fat
- ¼ cup parmesan cheese, grated
- 1 tablespoon dried Italian seasoning, low fat, low sodium
- ¼ cup crushed pork rinds

Directions:

1. Preheat your Toaster Oven to 425 degrees F in Bake Mode
2. Take a large baking dish and coat with ghee.
3. Pat chicken breasts dry and wraps with a towel.
4. Season with sunflower seeds and pepper.
5. Place in baking dish.

6. Take a small bowl and add mayonnaise, parmesan cheese, Italian seasoning.

7. Slather mayo mix evenly over chicken breast.

8. Sprinkle crushed pork rinds on top.

9. Bake for 20 minutes until topping is browned.

10. Serve and enjoy!

Nutritional Contents:

- Calories: 136
- Fat: 3g
- Carbohydrates: 1g
- Protein: 24g

Buffalo Chicken Lettuce Wraps

Serving: 2

Prep Time: 35 minutes

Cook Time: 10 minutes

Ingredients:

- 3 chicken breast, boneless and cubed
- 20 slices of almond butter lettuce leaves
- ¾ cup cherry tomatoes halved
- 1 avocado, chopped
- ¼ cup green onions, diced
- ½ a cup of ranch dressing
- ¾ cup hot sauce

Directions:

1. Take a mixing bowl and add chicken cubes and hot sauce, mix.

2. Place in the fridge and let it marinate for 30 minutes.

3. Preheat your Toaster Oven to 400 degrees Fahrenheit in Toast Mode

4. Place coated chicken on a cookie pan and bake for 9 minutes.

5. Assemble lettuce serving cups with equal amounts of lettuce, green onions, tomatoes, ranch dressing, and cubed chicken.

6. Serve and enjoy!

Nutritional Contents:

- Calories: 136
- Fat: 3g
- Carbohydrates: 1g
- Protein: 24g

Hearty Lemon And Pepper Chicken

Serving: 4

Prep Time: 5 minutes

Cook Time: 15 minutes

Ingredients:

- 2 teaspoons olive oil
- 1 and ¼ pounds skinless chicken cutlets
- 2 whole eggs
- ¼ cup panko
- 1 tablespoon lemon pepper
- Sunflower seeds and pepper to taste
- 3 cups green beans
- ¼ cup parmesan cheese
- ¼ teaspoon garlic powder

Directions

1. Pre-heat your Toaster Oven to 425 degrees F in Bake Mode
2. Take a bowl and stir in seasoning, parmesan, lemon pepper, garlic powder, panko
3. Whisk eggs in another bowl
4. Coat cutlets in eggs and press into panko mix

5. Transfer coated chicken to a parchment-lined a baking sheet

6. Toss the beans in oil, pepper, and sunflower seeds, lay them on the side of the baking sheet

7. Bake for 15 minutes

8. Enjoy!

Nutritional Contents:

- Calories: 136
- Fat: 3g
- Carbohydrates: 1g
- Protein: 24g

Balsamic Chicken And Vegetables

Serving: 2

Prep Time: 15 minutes

Cook Time: 25 minutes

Ingredients:

- 4 chicken thigh, boneless and skinless
- 5 stalks of asparagus, halved
- 1 pepper, cut in chunks
- 1/2 red onion, diced
- ½ a cup of carrots, sliced
- 1 garlic cloves, minced
- 2-ounces mushrooms, diced
- A ¼ cup of balsamic vinegar
- 1 tablespoon of olive oil
- ½ a teaspoon of stevia
- ½ tablespoon of oregano
- Sunflower seeds and pepper as needed

Directions:

1. Pre-heat your Toaster Oven to 425 degrees Fahrenheit in Bake Mode

2. Take a bowl and add all of the vegetables and mix

3. Add spices and oil and mix

4. Dip the chicken pieces into spice mix and coat them well

5. Place the veggies and chicken onto a pan in a single layer

6. Cook for 25 minutes.

7. Serve and enjoy!

Nutritional Contents:

- Calories: 136
- Fat: 3g
- Carbohydrates: 1g
- Protein: 24g

Cheesy Chicken Bits

Serving: 4

Prep Time: 10 minutes

Cook Time: 10 minutes

Ingredients:

- 2 pieces of 8 ounces chicken breast with the fat trimmed and sliced up in half (making 4 portions)
- 6 tablespoons of seasoned breadcrumbs
- 2 tablespoons of grated parmesan
- 1 tablespoon of melted butter

- Tablespoon of low-fat mozzarella cheese
- ½ a cup of marinara sauce
- Cooking spray as needed

Directions:

1. Pre-heat your Toaster Oven to 390 degrees Fahrenheit for about 9 minutes in Air Fry mode
2. Take the cooking basket and spray it evenly with cooking spray
3. Take a small bowl and add breadcrumbs and parmesan cheese
4. Mix them well
5. Take another bowl and add the butter, melt it in your microwave
6. Brush the chicken pieces with the butter and dredge them into the breadcrumb mix
7. Once the fryer is ready, place 2 pieces of your prepared chicken breast and spray the top a bit of oil
8. Cook for about 6 minutes
9. Turn them over and top them up with 1 tablespoon of Marinara and 1 and a ½ tablespoon of shredded mozzarella
10. Cook for 3 minutes more until the cheese has completely melted
11. Keep the cooked breasts on the side and repeat with the remaining pieces

Nutritional Contents:

- Calories: 251
- Carbohydrate: 14g
- Protein: 31g
- Fat: 9.5g

Crusty Sage Chicken Escallops

Serving: 4

Prep Time: 10 minutes

Cook Time: 50 minutes

Ingredients:

- 4 skinless chicken breast
- 2 and a ½ ounce of panko breadcrumbs
- 1 ounce of grated parmesan
- 6 pieces of finely chopped sage leaves

- 1 and a ¾ ounce of plain flour
- 2 beaten eggs

Directions:

1. Place the chicken between cling film and beat it roughly using a rolling pin to and give it a thickness of ½ cm

2. Take a bowl and add parmesan, sage, and breadcrumbs

3. Take another bowl and add flour and season with salt

4. Dredge the chicken in the seasoned flour followed by dredging them in the beaten egg and finally in the breadcrumbs mix

5. Pre-heat your Toaster Oven to a temperature of 392 degrees Fahrenheit in Air Fry mode

6. Take your cooking basket and spray it well

7. Spray the chicken with some oil as well

8. Place two of the pieces at a time in your cooking basket and cook for 4 minutes until a golden texture is seen

9. Once done, serve with a green salad

10. Enjoy!

Nutritional Contents:

- Calories: 363
- Carbohydrate: 35g
- Protein: 50g
- Fat: 5g

Crazy English Buttermilk Chicken

Serving: 4

Prep Time: 10 minutes

Cook Time: 20 minutes

Ingredients:

- 6 pieces of chicken thigh (skin on and bone-in)
- 2 cups buttermilk
- 2 teaspoon salt
- 2 teaspoon black pepper
- 1 teaspoon cayenne pepper

- 2 cups all-purpose flour
- 1 tablespoon baking powder
- 1 tablespoon garlic powder
- 1 tablespoon paprika
- 1 tablespoon salt

Directions:

1. Rinse your chicken thoroughly and remove any excess fat
2. Pat the chicken pieces dry
3. Take a large-sized bowl and add the chicken
4. Season with paprika, salt, and black pepper
5. Toss them well
6. Allow the chicken to marinate overnight (in the fridge)
7. Pre-heat your Toaster Oven to a temperature of 400 degrees Fahrenheit in Air Fry mode
8. Take a bowl and add pepper, flour, salt and paprika
9. Coat the chicken with the mixture
10. Arrange them in a single layer on your cooking basket and cook for about 10 minutes
11. Keep repeating the process until all of the chicken are cooked
12. Enjoy!

Nutritional Contents:

- Calories: 282
- Carbohydrate: 3g
- Protein: 55g
- Fat: 4g

True Korean BBQ Satay

Serving: 4

Prep Time: 10 minutes

Cook Time: 10 minutes

Ingredients:

- 3/4rth ounces of boneless and skinless chicken tenders
- ½ cup of low sodium soy sauce
- ½ cup of pineapple juice

- 1/4th cup of sesame oil
- 4 cloves of chopped up garlic
- 4 chopped up scallions
- 1 tablespoon of freshly grated ginger
- 2 teaspoon of toasted sesame seeds
- 1 pinch of black pepper

Directions:

1. Skewer the chicken pieces into the skewers and trim down any excess fat

2. Take a large bowl and add the remaining ingredients

3. Dip the skewered chicken into the bowl

4. Allow them to marinate for about 2-24 hours

5. Preheat your Toaster Oven to 390 degrees Fahrenheit in Air Fry mode

6. Remove the chicken and place it on a towel to dry

7. Place them on your cooking basket and cook for 5-7 minutes

8. Enjoy!

Nutritional Contents:

- Calories: 361
- Carbohydrate: 37g
- Protein: 26g
- Fat: 12g

Garlic And Lemon Salmon

Serving: 4

Prep Time: 10 minutes

Cook Time: 15 minutes

Ingredients:

- 3 ounces butter
- 1 tablespoon parsley
- 1 tablespoon dill
- 1 tablespoon lemon, minced
- 6 salmon fillets

Directions:

1. Heat all ingredients over a saucepan over medium heat except salmon, add salmon fillets and coat them well
2. The air fryer toaster oven should be preheated at 350 F for 5 min.
3. The basket should be covered by aluminum foil.
4. The salmons are placed in the basket and baked for 15 min with intermittent flipping and brushing of butter until they turn crispy and brown.
5. The dish is served hot.

Nutritional Contents:

- Calories: 350
- Fat: 41g
- Carbohydrates: 20g
- Protein: 28g

Chipotle Tuna Melt

Serving: 4

Prep Time: 10 minutes

Cook Time: 5 minutes

Ingredients:

- 1 slice American cheese
- 12 ounces tuna
- ¼ tablespoon cilantro
- ¼ tablespoon pepper
- 3 ounces butter
- 2 chipotle pepper, in adobo sauce
- ¼ tablespoon garlic sault
- 2 slices Italian bread
- ½ cup mayonnaise

Directions:

1. The mayonnaise, garlic salt, chipotle peppers, pepper, and cilantro, are mixed
2. in a bowl to which the tuna should be added. The bread slices are coated with butter on which the tuna mixture is spread.

3. The mixture is topped with a slice of cheese and finally covered with another slice of butter coated bread to form a sandwich.
4. The air fryer toaster oven should be preheated at 320 F for 5 min.
5. The basket should be covered by aluminum foil.
6. The sandwich is placed in the basket and baked for 5 min with intermittent flipping until cheese melts, and the bread turns brown.
7. The dish is served hot.

Nutritional Contents:

- Calories: 365
- Fat: 13g
- Carbohydrates: 40g
- Protein: 43g

Coconut Shrimp Mix

Serving: 4

Prep Time: 10 minutes

Cook Time: 8 minutes

Ingredients:

- 1 tablespoon cilantro
- ¼ cup lime juice
- 1 Serrano chili, sliced
- 2 cups flaked coconut

- ¼ cup honey
- ½ cup panko
- 12 ounces shrimp, shelled
- 1 tablespoon pepper
- ¼ tablespoon salt
- ½ cup flour
- 2 whole eggs

Directions:

1. The flour and pepper should be mixed in a bowl, and eggs are beaten in another bowl.
2. Panko and coconut are mixed in the third bowl.
3. The shrimp is coated with the flour, egg and finally dredged in the panko coconut mixture.
4. The air fryer toaster oven should be preheated at 390 F for 5 min. The basket should be covered by aluminum foil.
5. The shrimps are placed in the basket and air fried for 8 min with intermittent flipping.
6. The sauce is prepared by mixing lime juice, honey, and Serrano chili.
7. Serve shrimp with prepare sauce, enjoy!

Nutritional Contents:

- Calories: 250
- Fat: 8g
- Carbohydrates: 30g
- Protein: 17g

Healthy Fish Crumbs

Serving: 4

Prep Time: 10 minutes

Cook Time: 12 minutes

Ingredients:

- 4 strips (1 pound cod)
- ½ tablespoon pepper
- 1 tablespoon bay seasoning
- ½ tablespoon salt
- 3 tablespoon tartar sauce
- ½ cup flour
- 2 cups breadcrumbs
- 4 slices lemon wedges
- 2 eggs, beaten

Directions:

1. Cover the fish with salt and pepper.
2. The breadcrumbs mixed with old bay, egg, and flour are placed in three different bowls.
3. Coat the fish with flour, egg, fish, flour
4. Pre-heat your Toaster Oven to 390 degrees F
5. The basket should be covered by aluminum foil.

6. The fish are placed in the basket and heated for 12 min with intermittent flipping.

7. The fish should be removed from the basket and served with sauce and lemon.

Nutritional Contents:

- Calories: 354
- Fat: 22g
- Carbohydrates: 26g
- Protein: 10g

Tuna Patties

Serving: 4

Prep Time: 10 minutes

Cook Time: 10 minutes

Ingredients:

- 1 and1/2 tablespoons almond flour
- ½ lemon, juiced

- 1 teaspoon dried dill
- 1 and ½ tablespoon mayo
- 2 cans tuna, packed in water
- Salt and pepper to taste
- ½ teaspoon onion powder
- 1 teaspoon garlic powder

Directions:

1. Set your Toaster Oven on Air fryer mode to 390 degrees F for 12 minutes.
2. Combine the tuna with all other ingredients and form 4 equal-sized patties.
3. Place the tuna patties on the cooking tray.
4. Transfer to your Toaster Oven
5. Cook until the timer runs out, making sure to flip it about halfway through
6. Serve and enjoy!

Nutritional Contents:

- Calories: 338
- Fat: 4g
- Carbohydrates: 9g
- Protein: 15g

Southern Catfish

Serving: 4

Prep Time: 10 minutes

Cook Time: 14 minutes

Ingredients:

- ¼ teaspoon cayenne pepper
- ½ cup cornmeal
- ½ cup yellow mustard
- 1 lemon
- 1 cup milk
- 2 pounds catfish fillets
- ¼ teaspoon onion powder
- ¼ teaspoon garlic powder
- ¼ teaspoon chili powder
- ¼ teaspoon ground black pepper
- ½ teaspoon salt
- 2 tablespoons dried parsley flakes
- ¼ cup all-purpose flour

Directions:

1. Soak catfish in milk, squeeze lemon juice on top
2. Let it chill for 15 minutes
3. Set your Toaster Oven to 390 degrees F in Air Fry mode, with the timer set to 14 minutes
4. Rub catfish fillets with remaining ingredients and place on a cooking tray
5. Transfer to your Oven and let it cook until the timer runs out
6. Serve and enjoy!

Nutritional Contents:

- Calories: 231
- Fat: 20g
- Carbohydrates: 20g
- Protein: 14g

Lightning Source UK Ltd.
Milton Keynes UK
UKHW020812180621
385734UK00005B/145